MOM
Draw with Me!

A Mother & Daughter Doodle Book

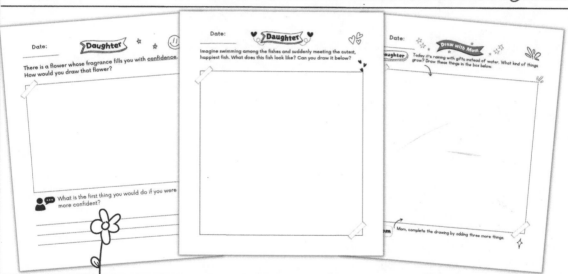

Christine Monroe
PASSIONLAND®

Questions and Customer Service:

Write to us at: **contact@passionland-books.com**

Follow us on
Instagram
@passionland.books

Hey there! Congratulations on starting your journey with "Mom, Draw with Me." As you and your daughter dive into this beautiful world of creativity, I have a special surprise just for you — a complimentary copy of the <u>Together Time e-Book</u>. This is our gift to you, a carefully crafted companion to your new journal that promises to enrich your bonding experience.

"Together Time" it's crafted specifically for mothers and daughters looking to truly enrich their relationship. Imagine having a guide that helps you dive deep into each other's worlds through beautifully designed journaling prompts, creative activities, and heartfelt discussions.

This isn't just any journal. It's a journey - a tool that grows with you both, adapting to your relationship's evolving needs. Whether you're navigating through a tough patch or celebrating the best times, this e-Book is like having a pathway to deeper connection right at your fingertips.

I genuinely believe this could be a beautiful, transformative experience for you and your daughter. It's such a unique way to strengthen your bond and create lasting memories.

Scan and <u>DOWNLOAD for FREE</u> TODAY!

Or
Acess the link below:
https://freebies.passionland-books.com/together-time

Why you absolutely need the Together Time e-Book:

Imagine having a secret toolbox, one that offers you and your daughter endless opportunities to laugh, learn, and connect on a deeper level.

<u>That's exactly what you'll find inside your free e-Book</u>:

- **Unlock New Adventures:** Beyond drawing, this e-Book introduces writing, storytelling, and crafting projects that will unlock new layers of creativity and communication between you.

- **Strengthen Your Bond:** Each activity is designed not just for fun, but to foster understanding and empathy. It's about turning the pages of this journal into a bridge that brings your hearts closer.

- **Capture Precious Moments:** With the Together Time e-Book, you'll create a living diary of unforgettable memories. It's not just about the time spent together; it's about enriching those moments with meaning and joy.

- **Effortlessly Integrate New Ideas:** The activities blend seamlessly into your journaling routine, each one a stepping stone to greater closeness and joy. They are simple, impactful, and designed to fit into your life with ease.

Scan and DOWNLOAD for FREE TODAY!

Or
Acess the link below:
https://freebies.passionland-books.com/together-time

Follow us on
Instagram
@passionland.books

About the author

Hey there! I'm **Christine Monroe**.

Living in the heartbeat of New York with my two spirited kids, I'm on a beautiful, whirlwind adventure called parenthood. Every day with my children is a dance between chaos and joy, filled with unexpected lessons and lots of laughter. Our home is our playground, a place where we create, learn, and sometimes just make a big mess!

Being a mom has taught me more about life than anything else ever could. It's about those little moments—like baking cookies at midnight or our long walks in the rain, where the world around us fades and we just talk and laugh. These are the times that truly define us. I've learned that parenting isn't about guiding from the sidelines; it's about jumping into the game, getting your hands dirty, and learning alongside them.

On this journey, I've realized that my greatest role as a mom is to provide a safe space where my kids can grow and express themselves freely. It's about showing up, being present, and loving fiercely. Through my stories, I hope to connect with you - other parents navigating this challenging, rewarding path - sharing insights and embracing the beauty of raising humans.

Let's celebrate the messy, beautiful art of raising children together. Join me here for real stories from a real mom, navigating real life.

About the book

It's time to let your imagination run wild!

"Mom, Draw with Me!" is a super-cute and imaginative multi-chapter book where you and Mom draw and color together.

Together you will discover fun things to draw, but also beautiful or even touching memories that you have shared.

It is essential to be creative and not overthink about what your drawing will look like - just draw and enjoy every moment.

There are also some pages where you have to write a few words about your drawings (to lighten the mood and start funny or even touching and exciting conversations).

Be careful! Some chapters are designed for you to draw separately (each of you has your own drawing to do), while others invite you both to draw on the same page - usually to complement each other's drawings.

In this case, it is very important to leave space on the page for each of you.

A messege for mom...

So... why draw together?

Well, drawing together can be a fun and bonding activity for mothers and daughters. It can help improve communication and the emotional connection between the two of you.

Drawing and creating art together can also be a way for you (as a mother) to learn more about your daughter's interests and passions.

Why? Because children often feel more comfortable expressing themselves through art than through verbal communication, so drawing together can be an effective way for you to understand your daughter's thoughts and feelings.

It can also be a great way for you to encourage your daughter's creativity and imagination. We all know that children often have a natural inclination to be curious and explore the world around them, and of course, drawing is an advantage because it can be a great way to channel that curiosity and creativity.

Overall, drawing together can be a great way for parents and children to connect, learn, and grow together. It can be a fun and rewarding activity for both you and your daughter and can lead to a deeper understanding and appreciation of each other.

That said, I wish you many happy moments together that will bring you closer, and strengthen your relationship as you go through this book.

This Doodle Book Belongs to:

AND

This book is all about building a wise, open, and powerful relationship between a mother and her daughter. Be imaginative, be as creative as you can, let your feelings come out, and enjoy every moment you spend together. This is probably one of the best tools you have to strengthen your mother-daughter relationship. Use it wisely and cherish it as the years go by.

The Mother-Daughter Doodle Book

Start Date

End Date

TABLE OF
CONTENTS

CHAPTER 1
Draw and Write

This chapter challenges you both to draw and to put into words how you feel about your drawings.

Follow the instructions written on each page and feel free to write absolutely anything that comes to mind.

If you found difficult to express yourself in writing or drawing, ask each other for advice. You may come up with new ideas that will challenge your imagination. It could be fun!

Daughter

There is a flower whose fragrance fills you with <u>confidence</u>. How would you draw that kind of flower?

What is the first thing you would do if you were more confident?

_____

_____

_____

Date:

_____

Mom

There is a flower whose fragrance fills you with <u>gratitude</u>. How would you draw that kind of flower?

What are you most grateful for?

_____

_____

_____

Date: _____

You found a small box filled with courage. Can you draw the box below?

What can you do with this box?

_____

_____

_____

_____

Mom

You found a small box filled with honesty. Can you draw the box below?

What can you do with this box?

_____

_____

_____

Date:

_____

You discovered a secret place filled with peace and serenity. What is it look like?

What does peace mean to you?

_____

_____

_____

Mom

You have discovered a secret place full of love and romance. What is it look like?

What does love mean to you?

Date:

_____

You have the ability to create a superhero. What does the hero you create look like?

What powers does the hero you created have?

_____

_____

_____

Date: _____

Mom

You have the ability to turn a villain into a good person. What does this person look like after the transformation?

What new qualities does this person have?

_____

_____

_____

Date:

_____

Someone left a big box of surprises at your front door just for fun. Draw this box below.

What kind of delights awaits you in this amazing package?

_____

_____

_____

Date:
_____

Mom

Imagine your favorite animal as the mayor of a town. What would it look like in its mayor outfit?

Write three rules it would make to keep all the animals happy.

_____

_____

_____

CHAPTER 2
Draw Together

Also called the "interactive chapter".

Even though you have to be more careful because you have to give each other space to draw on the same box, it can be very educational and fun to create a drawing together.

Pay attention to the instructions you'll find on each page and make sure you talk to each other before you start drawing.

It's important to know what the other is thinking and how much space each of you needs to draw.

I hope this chapter will kick-start important conversations in your relationship and give you quality time to spend and enjoy together.

Date:

Draw with Mom

 Daughter Imagine a day without tears, grief, envy and hunger. What does this day look like? Maybe it looks like love?

 **Mom** Add one thing that can make that day even more special. Also, explain to your daughter why you chose it and what it means to you.

Date:

Draw with Mom

Daughter

Imagine that on a very clear night, the stars revealed a secret message just for you. Try to represent it in the box below.

Mom

What do you think about the secret message your daughter received? Do you have your own secret that can be drawn alongside your daughter's?

Date:

_____

Daughter

Today it's raining with gifts instead of water. What kind of things grow? Draw these things in the box below.

Mom Complete the drawing by adding three more things.

Date:
_____

Daughter Draw a picture of a place that exists in your imagination.
Think of three things that best represent this place.

_____
_____
_____

Mom This time you don't have to draw. Instead, you have to
guess what this place is and write a story about it.

Draw with Mom

Daughter It's burger night! Draw the biggest burger you've ever seen.

Mom Draw your favorite sauce on top of the burger.

Date:
_____

Daughter You have a fashion dress agency. Can you design your favorite dress in the box below?

Mom Can you draw your favorite dress pattern too? Try to make it different from your daughter's. When you have finished, vote for the one you like best, and give it 5 stars.

Draw with Mom

Daughter You're at the zoo and you see an animal you've never met before. What does this animal look like?

Mom Draw this animal's friends right next to it.

Date:

_____

Daughter You're in a cartoon and you're the most anticipated star. What kind of cartoon is it and what kind of artist are you?

 Mom You're in that scene too. Make sure you're standing right next to your daughter.

Date:

Daughter You're old enough to drive. What does your dream car look like? Draw your dream car in the box below.

Mom Give the car a color.

Date:
_____

Daughter You have been on a hiking trip in the mountains. What does the mountain you have climbed look like?

Mom Draw the rest of the people on the hike. Make sure you're among them.

Date:

Daughter Imagine a flying animal. What does this animal look like? Draw yourself riding this animal.

Mom Draw the eyes of this animal.

Date:
_____

Draw with Mom

Daughter You're twice your age. Draw yourself in the box below when you are twice your age.

Mom Draw yourself half the age you are now.

Date:
_____

Daughter

Look around and pick an object. Did you find it? Perfect! Now draw it.

Mom I want you to draw a face on this object.

Date:

_____

Daughter

Do you have a favorite book? Look at it carefully and try to make an alternative cover for your favorite book.

Mom Draw the back cover of this book, right next to the front cover that your daughter has drawn.

Date:

Daughter You're in the woods and you see an intricate, made-up flower. What this flower looks like?

Mom Can you make a bouquet with these kinds of flowers?

Date:

_____

Draw with Mom

Daughter

Think of the 3 most interesting animals you know. Try to combine these 3 animals to create your own mythical creature. Draw only the body.

Mom

It's your turn. Draw the head of this mythical creature.

Draw with Mom

Daughter Imagine things that float. Fill half a page with them.

Mom You fill the other half.

Date: _____

Daughter

Imagine that you can create your own fruit. Draw a basket of your own fruit.

Mom

Draw these fresh fruits that have been cut in half next to your daughter's fruit basket.

Draw with Mom

Daughter Imagine a wolf made of branches. What does this wolf look like?

Mom Use your imagination and draw something on the wolf's branches.

Date:

_____

Daughter Imagine what a perfect fish tank looks like. Can you draw it in the box below?

Mom In the fish tank your daughter has drawn, draw some of the fish's friends.

Date: _____

Daughter

Imagine a pair of magical boots that can take you to any place you think of instantly.

Mom

Draw the place you think your daughter is thinking of.

CHAPTER 3
"Imagine"

I have mentioned the word imagination several times throughout this book.

Well, now it's time to let your imagination run wild and be as creative as possible.

This is the chapter where you have to imagine things and draw them.

You don't have to think about exactly what those things look like in reality, but what they look like in your imagination.

You may see different opinions and perspectives which you can then debate together.

Wish you lots of inspiration and fun!

Date:

Daughter

Imagine a powerful queen, dressed in a beautiful dress (or armor?)

Date:

_____

Imagine you have found a treasure. What does this treasure look like and what did you find inside?

Daughter

Imagine walking on a giant rainbow that has 10 colors. What does this rainbow look like?

Date:
_____

Mom

Imagine you are a magician with a magic wand. What would you do with it? What magical things can you create?

Date:

_____

Daughter

Imagine dinosaurs are alive today. What would the world and your life look like if dinosaurs roamed around?

Mom

Imagine a memory holder. Put something precious inside. Will it be a moment of happiness? A childhood wish? Or something else?

Daughter

Imagine a a flower growing out of a carrot growing out of a birthday cake.

Date:

Mom

_____

Imagine you have your own brand of noteBooks. Draw the logo for this brand.

Date:

_____

Daughter

Imagine you woke up one morning and you were a giant. What would you look like?

Date:

_____

Imagine living in the ocean for a day. What would your ocean home look like?

Date:

_____

Daughter

Imagine that you live in the universe. What is your home in the universe like?

Date:

Imagine your lunch consisted of nothing but flowers. What would it look like?

Daughter

Imagine being brave and courageous for a day. What would you do that day? Can you draw one thing you would do below?

Date:

_____

Imagine creating the next wonder of the world. What would that wonder be?

Date:

_____

Daughter

Imagine being able to change the weather every morning to suit your mood. What would today be like? Would it be sunny, cloudy, or gloomy?

Mom

Imagine a map with roads leading nowhere, curving all over the place, and funny town names.

Daughter

Think of the most interesting pair of shoes you would like to have. Decorate them and give them a different color. You can even print your favorite quote on them.

Date:

_____

Mom

Imagine that you found a magical door in your backyard that leads to another world. Sketch what lies on the other side of the door.

CHAPTER 4
Unleash your Creativity

"Unleash your creativity" means taking your imagination to the next level.

If in the previous chapter, you had to use your imagination, now it's time to use your creativity even more and create artistic designs according to the instructions on each page.

You can see this as a challenge to evolve and become more creative.

I wish you both the best of luck.

Date: _____

Think of a humble monk, dressed in a simple brown robe and no shoes. How would you draw this monk?

Mom

A muscular, scantily clad barbarian with a large beard and an unkempt haircut. He is armed, of course. Does he have a big axe or a big impressive sword?

Date:

_____

You're swimming among the fishes and suddenly meeting the cutest, happiest fish. What does this fish look like? Can you draw it below?

Date:

_____

Mom

Imagine that you could design a treehouse inspired by your favorite season. What unique elements would it have related to that season?

Date:

_____

Go back in time for a moment and remember the best holiday you ever had. Draw the one thing that reminds you the most of this holiday.

Imagine that you could grow a garden where each plant represents a different emotion. What would each plant look like?

Date:

_____

Think of a pair of pants running away from a shirt (and maybe some other clothes).

Think of a new type of tree that bears any kind of fruit you choose. What would it look like?

Date:

_____

Imagine a unicorn meeting a beautiful young maiden. He tosses his head gently as she caresses his mane. Can you draw this below?

Think of a mysterious lady holding her cat. But she's not just any lady, and neither is her cat. They both have bright and sneaky eyes.

CHAPTER 5
Randomly Drawings

This is the chapter where everything is random.

The nice thing about this chapter is that it's up to you who draws what.

Before you turn each page, decide who is going to draw, and then write the person responsible (mom/daughter) in the box at the top of each page.

You might come up with a difficult drawing or a very easy one. It depends on each person's luck.

Remember, you don't have to follow any rules. Just follow the instructions on the page and have fun spending quality time together.

Date:

_____

Draw a t-shirt you'd love to wear.

Date:

_____

Draw a llama surfing.

Date:

_____

Draw a mysterious stairway. Where does it lead to?

Date:

_____

Draw an animal with arms instead of legs and feet instead of arms.

Date:

_____

Draw a dinosaur crying.

Draw a circus elephant standing on a ball.

Draw a cat chasing a dog.

Draw a flamingo doing ballet.

Draw a rainstorm of sprinkles.

Draw a food eating another food.

Date:

_____

Draw a walking taco.

Date:

_____

Draw a donut riding a skateboard.

Date:
_____

Draw a cheeseburger wearing a dress.

Draw a lemon making orange juice.

Date:
_____

Draw your favorite teacher as a zombie.

Date:

_____

Draw yourself as a fairy.

Draw a troll riding a unicorn.

Date:

_____

Draw a dragon breathing rainbows.

Draw an elf jumping on a trampoline.

Date:

_____

Draw a rocket ship traveling to a candy planet.

Date:

_____

Draw a parade with animals playing musical instruments.

Date:

_____

Draw a sweater made out of candy.

Draw a pair of shoes made out of flowers.

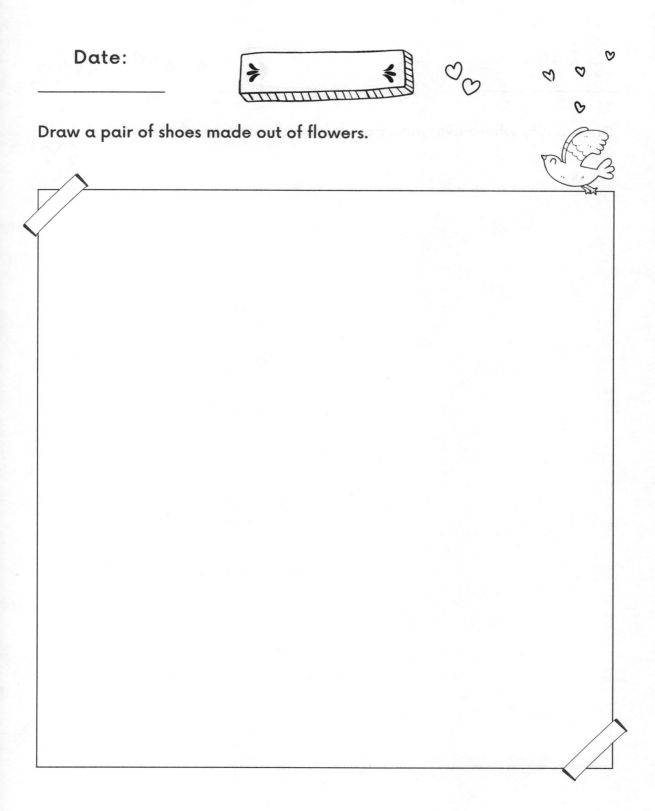

Date:

_____

Draw a city where everyone travels by balloon instead of cars.

Draw a friendly monster who is the guardian of your closet and keeps all the scary things away.

Date:

_____

Draw a magical ice cream shop where the scoops can float and choose their own toppings.

Date:
_____

Draw something gross.

Date:

_____

Draw a library where the books can talk and walk around. What stories do they tell each other?

CHAPTER 6
Draw Together – Advanced

This chapter will challenge you both on the drawing side and in expressing in words how you feel about your drawing.

Follow the instructions on each page. Feel free to write anything that comes to mind.

If you find it difficult to express yourself in writing or drawing, ask each other for advice. You might come up with new ideas that challenge your imagination. It could be fun!

Date:

_____

Daughter Without looking at the paper, draw any object, such as your own hand, on a continuous line without lifting your hand from the page.

Mom Do the exact same thing, right next to your daughter's drawing.

Daughter Randomly select three words and draw what they mean together.

Mom Do the exact same thing, right next to your daughter's drawing.

Daughter Draw a towel in a crumpled position.

Mom Draw a towel strewn on the ground.

Date:
_____

Daughter Draw the ingredients of your next meal before you prepare it.

Mom Draw the meal you have prepared together.

Date:

_____

Daughter Draw a secret base on the moon.

Mom What fun gadgets are inside? Can you draw them?

Date:

_____

Daughter Draw something BIG.

Mom Draw something small.

Date:

_____

Daughter Create a drawing using only circles.

Mom Create a drawing using only lines.

Date:
_____

Daughter : Create your own birthday cake.

 Mom : Draw the candles on your daughter's cake.

Date:

☼ Mom & Daughter - Together ☼

Daughter Draw a new emoji.

Mom Draw a new emoji, next to your daughter's.

Date:

_____

Daughter Draw 3 different types of flowers.

 Mom Draw another 3 types, right next to the ones your daughter drew.

Date:

_____

Daughter Draw one thing that starts with the first letter of your name.

Mom Can you do the same?

✣ Mom & Daughter - Together ✣

Daughter Draw your mom wearing a stack of hats.

Mom Color each hat drawn by your daughter with different colors.

Date:
_____

Daughter Draw the strangest pair of glasses you can imagine.

Mom Draw a face that matches the glasses drawn by your daughter.

⚘ Mom & Daughter - Together ⚘

Daughter Draw a human scissor.

Mom Draw her pair.

Date:

☼ Mom & Daughter - Together ☼

Daughter Draw a snowman wearing only a hat.

Mom Add minimum 5 accessories to the snowman drawn by your daughter.

Date:
_____

☼ Mom & Daughter - Together ☼

Daughter Draw a tall tower of your favorite foods.

 Draw your daughter looking up at it.

Date:

Daughter Draw a colorful, striped bicycle with ten seats and twelve wheels.

Mom Draw yourself riding that bike.

☼ Mom & Daughter – Together ☼

Daughter Draw an octopus.

Mom Make sure the octopus is wearing high heels.

A Heartfelt Thank You From Christine Monroe

Dear Wonderful Mom and Daughter,

You did it! You've reached the end of "**Mom, Draw with Me**" and I can't express how grateful I am that you chose to embark on this creative adventure together.

It warms my heart to think of all the laughter, the shared stories, and the beautiful drawings that have now filled the pages of this book, bringing you closer together. As an author, my greatest joy comes from knowing that my work has genuinely contributed to creating memorable moments.

Thank you for letting me be a part of your journey toward a stronger, happier relationship. Every line you've drawn and every color you've chosen has turned this book into a treasure chest of precious memories.

If this book has touched your life, could I ask you to share your experience? A review on Amazon would mean the world to me. It not only helps our book reach other families like yours but also lets them see the potential impact they can enjoy. If you could include a picture or video of some of your favorite drawings, that would be even more incredible!

Thank you once again from the bottom of my heart. Keep those colors bright and those bonds strong. Here's to more drawing, more laughing, and more loving.

With all my love and gratitude,
Christine Monroe

Don't Forget Your **FREE** Resource!

Scan and **DOWNLOAD for FREE** TODAY!

Or
Acess the link below:
https://freebies.passionland-books.com/together-time

Follow us on
Instagram
@passionland.books

How to Get Your Free e-Book:

Simply scan the QR code found on this page, and you'll be directed to download your free copy of the Together Time e-Book. It's our way of saying thank you for inviting us into your family's journey.

I believe every mother and daughter deserve stories filled with laughter, love, and understanding. This e-Book is more than a companion; it's a gateway to experiences that you will cherish for years to come.

So why wait? _Scan_, _download_, and discover all the incredible ways you can grow closer every day. Your most memorable moments together start right here.

Join Me on Social Media for a Journey Toward <u>Stronger Family Bonds</u>

If you're passionate about nurturing healthier and happier relationships within your family, I warmly invite you to follow my social media pages. Every week, I share insights and resources that I've crafted specifically to help families like yours flourish. Here's what you can expect when you join our community:

- **Exclusive Content:** I love to share special tips, personal reflections, and inspiring stories that you won't find anywhere else. These are my little secrets to keeping family bonds strong, shared directly with you.

- **Weekly Inspiration:** From practical advice on everyday parenting challenges to creative activities that bring the family together, my posts are designed to provide ongoing support and fresh ideas for your family life.

- **Updates and Announcements:** Be the first to hear about my new projects, books, and workshops. I'm always working on something new to help your family succeed, and my social media followers are always the first to know!

Following me on social media is more than just updates; it's about becoming part of a family dedicated to growing and learning together. I'm here to support you every step of the way.

Let's connect and make family life even more wonderful. Follow me today and start enriching your family's journey!

With warmth and excitement,
Christine Monroe

@Passionland.books

Made in United States
Cleveland, OH
12 December 2024

11743183R00070